THE
TWELVE
COMMANDMENTS
OF
SUCCESS

EXPLORING THE PREDICTABILITY OF SUCCESS

MAYOWA OLUWAJOBI

The Twelve Commandments of Success

ISBN: 978-978-982-336-9

Table of Contents

Introduction

Success is a universal desire; it is the most desirable thing in the heart of man. We all long to be successful, to be in control or in charge of every occurrence of our lives.

The most important key to attain success in life is to know the meaning and measure of success. The true meaning of success goes beyond the common label of success, such as owning luxurious cars, having lots of money, piling up trophies, making achievements, and obtaining degrees.

Success can be defined as the status of having accomplished and achieved an aim or set objective. In other words, success is the satisfactory accomplishment, in the pursuit of a given purpose.

Being successful means the achievement of desired visions and planned goals. Furthermore, success can be a certain social status that describes a prosperous person that could also have gained fame for its favorable outcome. The dictionary describes success as the following: "attaining wealth, prosperity and/or fame".

The media and society have misled us into thinking that living a successful life means to be extraordinarily wealthy and powerful. They have framed the minds of many to equating money and power with success, but the true meaning of success goes far beyond the popular descriptions.

Success is, leading and living an impactful life, creating values, and making this world a better place for everyone. Success doesn't come cheap, it won't just fall on your laps; you have to go after it. If you want it more than anything else, chase it down!

Success does not happen by accident, neither does failure. It is 'intentional'. There are certain rules, principles or laws of nature that guarantee success, therefore, anyone who aspires to attain success must follow it.

"Put your heart, mind, intellect,and soul into even your smallest acts.This is the secret of success"
Swami Sivananda

CHAPTER 1: THOU SHALT KNOW WHAT YOU WANT

The most important key to achieve success in life is to know the meaning and measure of success. Success is beyond owning luxurious cars, having lots of money, piling up trophies, making achievements, and obtaining degrees.

The media and society have misled us in thinking living a successful life means to be extraordinarily wealthy and amassing a lot of tangibles. But the true meaning of success is leading and living an impactful life, creating values, and making this world a better place for everyone.

Find Out Why

No matter what you embark on in life, whether personal or business-related; there is a need for the 'why' question to be answered.

"Why" is the reason of purpose for the existence of a thing. Everything in life was created for a purpose, including you. You need to know the reason you want to attain success in life. When you don't know what you want and why you want it, you will be tossed around by every wind of opinions, hence, embarking on a journey to nowhere. A journey in futility.

Success according to Webster's dictionary is the correct or desired result of an attempt. Zig Ziglar, one of the most reputable modern-day experts on success, motivation, and leadership points out in his book *Born to Win!* That success cannot be defined in one sentence; instead, it is comprised of many things.

Here are some few definitions of success you can use to create a meaning for your own life:

- Success is always doing your best until you reach your maximum potential.

- Success is believing that you can.

- Success is helping others succeed.

- Success is learning something new each day.

- Success is persistence.

- Success is taking charge of your destiny.

- Success is resolute.

- Success is accepting a fall as a ladder.

- Success is overcoming fear.

- Success is passion-driven

Take a day or two off, a few hours at least, dig in deep, and examine yourself. Identify what you want out of life; there must be a goal which, more than anything else, you desire to reach. Find out what it is, and how to get to your desired end. Knowing where you want to go gives your life a guiding or motivating purpose.

Adjust Yourself

We are all enclosed by events that we have no control over. We meet with people in different shades, colors, and backgrounds whose opinions and prejudices that you cannot move.

That is the reality of life; all you need do is adjusting yourself to it. The sailor makes his boat go on to its destination by adjusting the sails to the wind.

In rush hour traffic, you may need to change course, make some detours here and there, but you're still trying to get to the same definition. Don't be stuck in traffic.

Remember that there are variables that you can't control that would come your way in life. But you can control how you react to such situations.

Give attention to feedback. Listen to constructive criticism; it can help you identify areas where you need improvement.

Accept failure on the way of success. It is quite impossible to achieve success without stumbling at one point or the other along the way.

Always Challenge Yourself

In order to make the most of life, challenge yourself. You can't fulfill or achieve that dream by being stuck to your comfort zone. Resolve to always challenge yourself to pursue those goals that will stretch you. The more you challenge yourself, the greater your confidence becomes to challenge yourself yet again. Challenges help you grow in knowledge, skill and help you develop the capacity to believe more in your own ability.

Don't Compare Yourself with Others

You will lose sight of your goals and drift off the paths of success when you compare your success rate with that of others. Don't focus too much on what others are doing or not doing, unless it drives you on your own path of success; though the competition is healthy, putting much attention on it can lead you to internalize unhealthy attitudes.

When you derive a sense of pleasure or satisfaction from comparing your success to others', you are no longer the master of your own destiny. No matter what others are thinking or doing, let your self-worth brew from within.

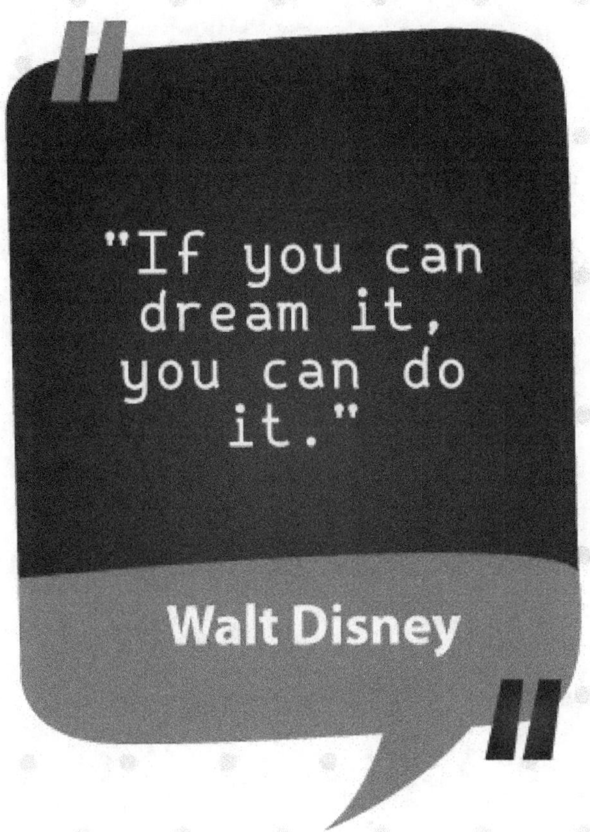

"If you can dream it, you can do it."
Walt Disney

CHAPTER 2: THOU SHALT DREAM BIG

Dare to get out of your comfort zone and try your hands on doing the impossible. Venturing into unfamiliar grounds stretches you and shows what you can become.

Expand your horizon, stretch your mind and expectations, enlarge the amount of work beyond what you would ordinarily do, and bend your imagination to the elastic limit.

Go to It

"Success doesn't come to you, you go to it." **Maria Collins**

Success doesn't come cheap, it won't just fall on your laps; you have to go after it. If you want it more than anything else, then chase it down.

Laziness will keep you far away from success, only those who are willing to "go to it" succeed.

Watch out for new opportunities, try new ventures, take risks and challenge yourself as much as you can. That's how you improve and measure growth; feeling free and filled with a zest for life.

Be Excellent

Excellence is required on the pathway to success. To be the best, you must offer the best. You must provide to others what they cannot get from anywhere else.

To attain success, run after excellence. Don't tackle a task haphazardly, do your best to bring the great out of it. Identify the skills that are of value to you, family, and society; work on building on it to attract the success you crave for.

Do it Now

Success is having the knowledge and understanding that you are in charge of your destiny. Your success is not dependent on external factors but is totally dependent on you and how you effectively adjust and navigate through those externalities.

Don't be a showboat; let your accomplishment announce you. Take responsibility for your actions, own up to your mistakes. Don't try to pass on the blame, or get defensive about it. Instead, simply accept and acknowledge it, and use such an incident as a learning experience for future purposes. As important as it is to own up to your errors, don't beat yourself up over them. Ensure to uncover the lesson of what you can do differently next time, and move on.

"I visualized where I wanted to be,what kind of player I wanted to become. I knew exactly where I wanted to go, and I focused on getting there."
Michael Jordan

CHAPTER 3: THOU SHALT CREATE A PLAN

Once you can identify your destination, and you have accepted the responsibility of getting there, you need to align yourself with an action plan. That is, you have got to plot out your route to your desired end.

Create a Vision

"The vision that you glorify in your mind, the ideal that you enthroned in your heart–this you will build your life by, and then you will become."
James Allen

You must have clarity of what you are about to achieve. If you can visualize it, then you can pursue it and achieve it.

Vision is seeing the end of a goal or purpose, then walking or running towards it. Success is all about creating values, bringing answers and solutions to the problems that people are struggling with.

Look for Problems to Solve

Look around and try to think of ways you can contribute to the society. What are people struggling with or complaining about? How can you make life easier for them in an effective way? Can you create a product or provide a service that fills a critical gap? Common problems include:

- *Social problems.* Can you think of a similar social problem that needs reinventing? For example, social media reinvented the way people interact with one another.

- *Technology problems.* Can you help people use technology to accomplish what they need to do? For example, technology companies design smaller and more powerful computer processors to improve the user experience.

- *Strategic problems.* Can you help someone else solve a strategic problem? For example, consultants help other companies and individuals become more productive, profitable, and prudent.

- *Interpersonal problems.* Can you help people get along with one another? For example, psychologists and marriage counselors help other people navigate the complex web of personal relationships. [a]

Procrastination

Many have come to believe that procrastination is the enemy of success, for most people, it is synonymous to laziness. But procrastination can be helpful when used strategically.

Procrastination can be described as using fear as a motivator. It could either be passive or active.

Passive procrastination is when we keep putting things off to tomorrow, the next day and the next, and so on. This is bad for your success rate; it can destroy your productivity and your work life, in general. Active procrastination, on the other hand, is when you are putting off a task for some time because you like the adrenalin rush that comes with working under pressure. This means you are actually doing what needs to be done in that time to get results that are more valuable.

We all procrastinate. Whether at work or at home, there are times when we put off things for later. Or should I say — not in the mood to do that thing? We don't even realize when procrastination gets stuck to our life like a leech and sucks productivity out of it. We simply put off things and are not doing anything at that time. It becomes a habit. As they say, old habits die hard but what if rather than giving up on this habit, we embrace this habit with a twist? This is where Active Procrastination comes into the picture. [b] Use procrastination positively!

Set SMART Goals

Ask yourself some critical questions about what you want to achieve out of life. Project for yourself where you want to be 5, 10, 15, or 20 years from now. Break it down into smaller chunks of specific goals; short and long term and adjust your goals periodically. Setting up goals gives you something to work towards and they help fill you with greater purpose.

Use the S.M.A.R.T formula to create achievable goals. S.M.A.R.T is an acronym for Specific, Measurable, Attainable, Realistic, and Time-bound. It is used by Life Coaches, Educators, Motivational Speakers, and Human Resource Departments for a system of goal setting and achievement. Each letter in S.M.A.R.T stands for an adjective that describes an effective way to set goals.

How to Use SMART

Paul J. Meyer, businessman, author, and founder of *Success Motivation International*, describes the characteristics of SMART goals in his 2003 book, *"Attitude Is Everything: If You Want to Succeed Above and Beyond."* We'll expand on his definitions to explore how to create, develop, and achieve your goals.

Specific

Your goal should be clear and specific; otherwise, you won't be able to achieve your focus. When drafting your goal, try to answer the five "W" questions:

- **What** do I want to accomplish?

- **Why** is this goal important?

- **Who** is involved?

- **Where** is it located?

- **Which** resources or limits are involved?

Measurable

It's important to have measurable goals so that you can track your progress and stay motivated. Assessing progress helps you to stay focused, meet your deadlines, and feel the excitement of getting closer to achieving your goal.

A measurable goal should address questions such as:

- How much?

- How many?

- How will I know when it is accomplished? (soon?)

Achievable

Your goal also needs to be realistic and attainable for it to be successful. In other words, it should stretch your abilities but still remain possible. When you set an achievable goal, you may be able to identify previously overlooked opportunities or resources that can bring you closer to it.

An achievable goal usually answers questions such as:

- How can I accomplish this goal?

- How realistic is the goal, based on other constraints, such as financial factors?

Tip:

Beware of setting goals that someone else has power over. For example, "Get that promotion!" depends on who else applies, and on the recruiter's decision. But "Get the experience and training that I need to be considered for that promotion" is entirely down to you.

Relevant

This step is about ensuring that your goal matters to you and that it also aligns with other relevant goals. We all need support and assistance in achieving our goals, but it is important to retain control over them. So, make sure that your plans drive everyone forward, but that you're still responsible for achieving your own goal.

A relevant goal can answer "yes" to these questions:

- Does this seem worthwhile?

- Is this the right time?

- Does this match our other efforts/needs?

- Am I the right person to reach this goal?

- Is it applicable in the current socio-economic environment?

Time-bound

Every goal needs a target date so that you have a deadline to focus on and something to work toward. This part of the SMART goal criteria helps to prevent everyday tasks from taking priority over your long-term goals.

A time-bound goal will usually answer these questions:

- When?

- What can I do six months from now?

- What can I do six weeks from now?

- What can I do today? [c]

Set Clear Priorities

At any given moment, you have a number of goals all in different states of completion. Deciding which goals are more important or time-sensitive than others is crucial. If you find yourself with too many goals, you're going to feel overwhelmed and are less likely to accomplish them. [d]

To be successful in life, you can't just distract yourself by staying busy or consuming aimless information online/offline. You need to work on constantly improving yourself.

"Success is
99% attitude
and 1%
aptitude."

Celestine Chua

CHAPTER 4: THOU SHALT CONTROL YOUR THOUGHTS

You need to have the belief that you can succeed. You are formed by your thought pattern; no one can stop you except you. You need to dedicate your mind to right thinking, though thoughts, like birds, fly over your head, you alone can decide the one that perches and build its nest on your head.

You must believe that you can control your thoughts and that your thoughts do not have to control you. Refuse to entertain depressing and destructive thoughts. Fear is an enemy of success; therefore flee from every thought of fear.

Always Maintain a Positive Mental Attitude

"Nothing can stop the man with the right mental attitude from achieving his goal; nothing on earth can help the man with the wrong mental attitude." **Thomas Jefferson**

Like the above quote says, you need to draw from a positive mentality and trust in your ability to succeed.

Cultivate the right mindset by replacing negative and toxic thoughts with the positive ones. You need to approach problems, not as roadblocks impeding your movement or obstacles stopping you, but as stepping stones to greater heights or merely as tasks that are needed to be completed for you to forge ahead. However, with the wrong mindset of fear, doubts, setbacks, people's opinion, and the like; you'll be much easier to stop.

Beat Negativity

The ride of success isn't a merry go round, on the pathway of success there's bound to be setbacks, challenges, difficulties, and moments that would make you doubt or question your commitment; these will always occur whether you're on the right path or wrong path.

Unclutter Your Mind

You don't really need anyone to help make you feel good, so, stop waiting for them. There may be a void in you longing to be filled, but another person won't fill it. You need to fix your relationship between yourself and the Creator first. Realize that with God, you are enough. Start loving, accepting, and appreciating yourself for who you are.

Get rid of the people in your life that only burden you with negativity, you don't need them. Focus on the essential things you have to do and ditch everything else that only keeps you busy. Get rid of thoughts that make you feel inferior, sad, jealous, anxious, fearful, angry, or frustrated.

Success should never be determined by the approval of others. If you try to please people to achieve success, you will live a highly disappointing life.

"Depending on what they are, our habits will either make us or break us. We become what we repeatedly do."
Sean Covey

CHAPTER 5: THOU SHALT ADOPT GOOD HABITS

Habits are things we do regularly without consciously thinking much about it. They shape your life more than you can possibly realize, they are often referred to as an automatic mental and behavioral activity. They make everyday life possible – either for good or bad.

More than 40 per cent of the actions you perform each day aren't actual decisions, but habits.

The habits you have picked up over the years are a reflection of what you do and where you are at the moment. If you are unhappy about where you are presently, you can gradually change by altering what you do daily. To achieve high levels of success in life, you must begin to develop the habits of the highly successful.

Among such habits are:

1. Focus on your strength: directing your strength and energy on high-value tasks rather than low-valued tasks brings the most reward.

2. First things first: the act of prioritizing your goals would make life easier for you. High achievers don't lose sight of what their major goal is. Don't minor in the major, or major in the minor.

3. Feed your mind: if you do nothing about the negative thoughts that are pumped into you, chances are you will be settling for less, at best average. Feeding your mind with positive thoughts will propel you towards leading a successful life. Don't call it quits when you have some setbacks or failure, instead harness the power of a positive mental attitude, strive to become a

better person, refine your skill-set, and invest in your future daily.

Establishing the Right Habits

Success is not stumbled upon by accident. It is borne out of adopting and adapting to positive or good habits and breaking away from negative behavioral patterns that can keep you away from accomplishing your dreams.

People who are successful in their work put to practice some of the good habits of successful people regularly, which other people don't. Therefore, if habits can make you successful, why not adopt the good habits of the highly successful people and list yourself among them.

Be committed to pursuing your God-given purpose; never lose sight of laying hold of something meaningful. In establishing the right habits that would lead you to achieve your dreams: identify the core values that make you tick, stay focused on your goals, build the right mindset, prioritize your goals, persevere, and set a deadline for your success.

Learn to Give

"Success isn't about how much money you make; it's about the difference you make in people's lives." **Michelle Obama**

One of the secrets to success is giving, and not receiving. A better way to get ahead in life is by being generous with that which you have.

Let us cut away from the competitive world of hoarding resources, and also break away from the dog-eat-dog mentality of climbing to the top. Helping others to get to the top will enable us to get to the point of success speedily.

Give your time, money, skills, and resources in helping others to be successful; there is great joy that will abound in your heart knowing you have helped to make a difference in the life of others.

"The difference between a successful person and others is not a lack of strength, not a lack of knowledge, but rather in a lack of will."
Vincent T. Lombardi

CHAPTER 6: THOU SHALT FOLLOW THROUGH

The ability to start something and follow through until you get it completed is a key to achieving long-term success. The more you project or picture yourself following through an important task, the more determined you will be to get it done.

"Your time is limited, so don't waste it living someone else's life. Don't be trapped by dogma - which is living with the results of other people's thinking. Don't let the noise of others' opinions drown out your own inner voice. And most important, have the courage to follow your heart and intuition, they somehow already know what you truly want to become. Everything else is secondary." **Steve Jobs**

Determination

Determination is the opposite of generalization; it is to have a fixed intention on a purpose and the willingness to work unceasingly towards that purpose in spite of any difficulties, barriers, or failures along the way. It takes quite a long time to achieve anything great. To keep the focus on a particular thing to wield success out of it does not just require being determined for a week, a month or a year; it takes multiple years, decades, and perhaps a lifetime or more to be the best at something. That's what it takes to achieve greatness.

Be Willing to Work Hard

"Unless you are willing to drench yourself in your work beyond the capacity of the average man, you are just not cut out for the positions at the top." **James Cash Penney**

True success is borne from work. You will never make it in life if you don't work towards your goal. Malcolm Gladwell describes in his book *Outliers*, an apparent phenomenon called the *"10,000-hour rule."*

As the name suggests, the 10,000-hour rule states that it takes 10,000 hours to master something. The rules hold true across a variety of fields ranging from writing to acting to music, sports, and the like.

You cannot become skilled at anything without putting a lot of time and effort into it. The more effort you put in achieving a goal, the better and faster you get it accomplished. Success requires maximum effort.

Will Power

"The difference between a successful person and others is not a lack of strength, not a lack of knowledge, but rather in a lack of will." **Vincent T. Lombardi**

Successful people aren't more intelligent or skilful than others, and they aren't necessarily stronger than others. The difference between them and the average person is that they have more desire and are tenacious than others. To succeed, you must be willing, more than you desire anything else.

Excellence

"No one ever attains very eminent success by simply doing what is required of him; it is the amount and excellence of what is over and above the required, that determines the greatness of ultimate distinction."
Charles Kendall Adams

Excellence is required on the path to success. To be the best, you must offer the best. You must provide to others what they can't get from anywhere else. Don't be a victim of multi-tasking. Focus and finish one project at a time, follow through on that which you have begun.

"Failure is simply the opportunity to begin again, this time more intelligently."
Henry Ford

CHAPTER 7: THOU SHALT OVERCOME FEAR AND FAILURE

Michael Jordan, one of the best the game of basketball has ever produced, in the prime of his career, was able to come to peace with how failure and losing games helped make him the player and the man that he became.

"I've missed more than 9000 shots in my career. I've lost almost 300 games. 26 times, I've been trusted to take the game-winning shot and missed. I've failed over and over and over again in my life. And that is why I succeed." **Michael Jordan**

Failure is neither fatal nor final, it is what you make out of it that determines where you end up on the pathway to success; it can either paralyze and keep you stagnant, or propel you towards achieving your goals. Failure isn't a badge of shame, but a call for self-reflection.

Don't Be Afraid of Failure or Fear

"Failure is simply the opportunity to begin again, this time more intelligently." **Henry Ford**

The story of Thomas Edison inventing the bulb was the result of hundreds of failed attempts, it's unconfirmed whether it actually happened or not, but we can draw a message from it:

In an interview, he was asked: "How do you feel after all of your failed attempts?"

His response was, "I didn't fail, I learned hundreds of ways not to invent a light bulb."

He saw each phase of "failure" as a lesson. He learned what won't work, and also might work instead, from that lesson. In every failure, there is a lesson. Pay attention to it, study them. Perhaps, you will learn how to succeed.

Discouragement

"Let no feeling of discouragement prey upon you, and in the end, you are sure to succeed." **Abraham Lincoln**

It is always appealing to quit when faced with discouragement, doubts, and setbacks. Don't pay attention to discouragement. If you are surrounded by doubts, ignore it.

Don't Stay Down

Life is going to knock you down sometimes, just get back up and dust yourself off. When life throws lemons at you, make lemonade out of it. Get the best out of every ugly situation.

Never hesitate to fail, since life gives many chances. What will define you is how you pick yourself up after you have fallen down. If your first attempt didn't work, don't give up or make excuses. Don't rationalize your failure by putting blame on someone or something else. Learn from your mistakes or failure, it is an opportunity for you to learn.

Be Courageous

"The worst thing that can happen to you is allowing yourself to die inside while you're still alive." **Anonymous**

Courage indeed is a virtue needed in your armor to obtain victory in the good fight for success. You will definitely be confronted with obstacles, challenges, and difficulties; you need the courage to forge on. Don't be afraid of others, no one can ruin you but yourself.

"All the money in the world can't buy you back good health."
Reba McEntire

CHAPTER 8: THOU SHALT TAKE CARE OF YOUR HEALTH

Success is taking good care of your physical, psychological, and spiritual needs. Success only comes with a well-balanced life; don't allow your health to suffer whilst gaining wealth, you might end up losing such wealth in the process of buying back your health.

Your environment has an incredible ability to shape your habits and behavior. By tweaking and making small changes to the physical environment around, you can make it much easier to cultivate and stick to good habits.

For instance, eating in smaller plates could make you eat less because bigger plates equal bigger portions and that means you eat more. Drinking soda or alcohol from slender glass, instead of short, fat ones could help cut down the intake of soda or alcohol. [a] Remember to put on your own oxygen mask before you assist others. Speak less so that you can listen more. Dress more simply, and eat less or healthier. Picture the most successful people in the world, they have a variety of traits that helped them become that way, including charisma, confidence, knowledge, and good instincts. Most often than not, you'll also find that they exercise and eat healthily.

Most successful people are not obese, and most of them will share their gym routine and diet with anyone who wants to know. Consider the following examples:

- Barack Obama worked out at least 45 minutes every single day before entering the Oval Office to get to work.

- Michelle Obama, the nation's most educated first lady, incorporates healthy foods into every meal and exercises daily, even if it means waking up at 4:30 a.m. to follow-through.

- Gwyneth Paltrow not only gets up at 4:30 a.m. to practice yoga, but she's also a major advocate for clean eating.

- Anna Wintour, the editor-in-chief for *Vogue* magazine, plays a vigorous tennis match for one hour each day before heading to work.

- Weatherman Al Roker says he eats a protein smoothie every day after his 7:30 weather segment.

Each of these people can boast of incredible accomplishments, and their healthy habits are a contributing factor. Anyone who aspires to live a successful lifestyle will benefit from being a little healthier. [b]

Cultivate a Healthy Lifestyle

In achieving new levels of productivity, treat your body well -- eat right, challenge your body, get proper sleep. Nutrition, exercise and sleep are keys to the success of those who perform at a high level.

Sleep is critical if you want to effectively lead a life of success. You need a clear head to navigate through the maze of life to hit a success. You owe it to yourself, family, and others to stay well-rested and alert. Ensure you structure your "pm" to get enough uninterrupted sleep, and your "am" so you can jump right out of bed to tackle your daily tasks adequately.

Engage your body in light exercises to keep your muscles strong and fit. Committing yourself to scheduled work-outs helps you to learn how to build resistance which results in personal growth and achievement. Eating right helps you to develop good habits. A healthy lifestyle accelerates your success rate.

Balanced Work and Life

*"There is an immutable conflict at work in life and in business, a constant battle between peace and chaos. Neither can be mastered, but both can be influenced. How you go about this is the key to success." **Phil Knight***

Finding a balance between your work and personal life can be a huge challenge in today's busy world. But it can be achieved if you can decide to work at it. Studies show that a poor work-life balance can result in unhappiness, unhealthy levels of stress, and reduced levels of productivity.

Here are a few tips that could help you out:

- Set your priorities

- Track your time

- Concentrate on one thing at a time

- Audit your habits and general lifestyle

- Ask for support

- Set boundaries

- Learn to say "No"

- Use technology for productive purposes

- Get plenty of exercises

- Find a mentor

Budgeting your Time and Money

On your way towards achieving success, time and money are important aspects that you can't easily discard. Take time to understand your income (in-flow) and expenses (outflow) in relation to your desired goals. You need to fit both resources into your current and future plan, to create solid stability for your perceived success. Make your time count. You have the same 24 hours in the day as everyone else does.

"It had long since come to my attention that people of accomplishment rarely sat back and let things happen to them. They went out and happened to things."
Leanardo Da Vinci

CHAPTER 9: THOU SHALT GO ON

Success is all about perseverance, not giving up. Perseverance creates grit, grit achieves success.

Be Good Sport

Successful ones choose their battles wisely; they have come to learn that losing a few battles can help you win a war. Success is celebrating small victories. Take time to celebrate anytime a goal is reached, and don't suck when you're on the losing side.

One of the secrets of success is knowing how to manage success. Walking is said to be a succession of falls and stumbles, life is a succession of failure and fumbles. Don't go on a pity party when you fail or lose, don't whine, complain, be sorry for yourself, or make other people sorry for you; get back up and get busy trying all over again.

Go the Extra Mile

"Success doesn't come to you, you go to it." **Maria Collins**

Success doesn't come cheap, it won't just fall on your laps; you have to go after it. If you want it more than anything else, chase it down. Laziness will keep you away from success, only those who are willing to "go to it" succeed.

"The greater danger for most of us lies not in setting our aim too high and falling short; by in setting our aim too low, and achieving our mark." **Michelangelo Buonarroti**

Many musicians of great repute spent years of their lives doing unpaid performances, the only reason they kept at it was that they loved to perform.

Put in Practice with Passion

Success is remembering to balance work with passion. The old cliché that *if you love what you do, you never have to work,* holds true at this instance. Work without passion builds up undue stress, toiling and empty achievements. To keep on practicing something over and over again, day in and day out for the years necessary to reach 10,000 hours is probably impossible except you are passionate about it.

There are times when despite your passion for what you are doing, you will not be in the mood to do it. When you don't feel like training, writing, or practicing, that's when you need the strength of self-discipline. Pick something you love to do, set your gaze on it, then create a practice schedule, and stick to it no matter whether you feel like it or not. Put your focus on what excites you.

Self-Discipline

Self-discipline begins from the mind. You need to take mastery of your own thoughts, in order to control your needs and desired goals. It helps you stay focused on reaching your goals, avoiding pitfalls, and overcoming obstacles and discomfort as you push yourself to new heights.

Self-Discipline is the ability to control your impulses, reactions, behaviors, and emotions. It allows you to let go of short-term gratification for long-term satisfaction. It helps you stop making excuses, get things done, stay focused, achieve mastery, and create productive habits.

"The most important single ingredient in the formula of success is knowing how to get along with people."
Theodore Roosevelt

CHAPTER 10: THOU SHALT CULTIVATE POSITIVE RELATIONSHIPS

If someone likes you, they would be willing to help you, but if someone doesn't like you, they may refuse to help or actively get in your way, impeding you.

Develop Good Communication Skills

Communication skills will help you on the way to leading a successful life. How well you can communicate can affect the impression others have of you and may make or break the opportunities you have towards your success goals.

- Resist saying the first thing on your mind. Instead, try waiting 5 seconds or so, and if you still think your input is relevant and contributes to the conversation, then voice your idea. [a]

- Understand your conversational objective(s) before you join a conversation.

- Be aware of yourself—not just your appearance (which is important), but also your words, your tone, and your body language. [b]

- If you're naturally shy or soft-spoken, challenge yourself to be more vocal and active in conversations. [c]

- Be empathetic towards others. If someone (a customer, a coworker, a manager, etc.) is having a hard time, be understanding. Put yourself in that person's place and try to think about what you might want to hear at that moment.

Teamwork

Scientific studies and practices have shown and proven that people that work harmoniously on a common goal, achieve more than one person on his own. This match up with the phrase: *"one shall chase a thousand, and two shall put ten thousand to flight"*

TEAM is an acronym that stands for 'Together Everyone Accomplishes More!' It is a fact, based on scientific and empirical studies, that people who work together with the focus on the same objectives, can accomplish more, than one person alone. Teamwork, therefore, is a key asset, together with the other principles, for cooperative success and common desired goals. [d]

Value Networking

"You can have everything in life you want if you will just help enough other people get what they want" **Zig Ziglar**

Networking is an important way to build and expand on success. Surround and connect yourself with people who are highly driven. You can bounce ideas off with such, and they can even link you up with other people. They can also motivate and support you through the process of getting to the top.

Study famous and successful people through their books, biographies, audiobooks, and lectures. Some of the most successful companies in recent times were created by brilliant pairs. Paul Allen and Bill Gates of Microsoft met in prep school, Larry Page and Sergey Brin of Google met in Stanford University, Steve Jobs and Steve Wozniak of Apple lived in the same neighborhood.

Surround yourself with the right people.

"Without consultation and wise advice, plans are frustrated, But with many counselors, they are established and succeed."

King Solomon

CHAPTER 11: THOU SHALT SEEK WISDOM

Successful people have the understanding that learning never stops. Wisdom is the principal thing, the most sought after commodity for lasting success, so the highly successful people pursue it with all their might and heart.

Learn to Ask

Don't go at it alone, equip yourself with good counsels. Without counsel purposes are disappointed: but in the multitude of counselors, they are established. [a] Discover your purpose by asking for counsel, then carry it out using all the help you can get. [b] Look around you, do you know someone who has the success that you have envisioned for yourself? Study what they are doing, how they approach life. Ask them for advice.

Avoid people who discourage or prevent you from reaching your destination. Don't allow them to feed your mind with wrong counsels that will hold you back on your way to success.

Find a Mentor

There are successful people who have been to where you are heading, reach out to them, don't be a lone ranger; one or two advice from them could save you from unnecessary hardships.

Mentoring could be attained directly or indirectly. You could find someone who is highly successful in what you plan to achieve, to help guide you step-by-step to your desired end; or you could search for materials such as tapes, videos, books, and the likes to help form a navigation system towards achieving your goals.

A mentor will help you network, troubleshoot, and strategize. Many people with a bit more experience than you are most likely willing to help you reach your goals, their satisfaction comes out of knowing that their guidance has helped breed success.

Learn to Be Kind

Be kind to everyone you meet along the way to success. You can offer help, smile, and be polite, no matter how they treat you. They might be passing through a hard patch, and what they need more than ever is a kind word or smile, which you can easily give to them. Being kind to others will not only make someone else's day, but it will also improve and make you feel better in return. Make it a goal to say one kind word to someone each day.

Learn As Much As You Can

Open your mind to learn new things, new information can help you make the right connections between ideas and use those ideas to make you attain success, and make your life better.

Expand your knowledge by reading books, biographies, taking online or offline courses, watching documentaries. Pursue subjects that are intriguing and interesting to you or will teach you a necessary skill.

Learn what helps successful people reach their goals. Learn as much as you can from 500 Fortune companies, industry, hobby, or goal in order to prop up your knowledge on how to succeed in life.

Ride on the Wings of Wisdom

The ancient Holy Book makes us understand the earth and all of its component, including the creation of man; which was wrought through Wisdom in the mind of an Intelligent Designer known as the Creator. Everything on earth and in the entirety of the universe functions through laid down laws and principles. For instance, a seed of orange cannot grow unless it is being planted in a medium called soil. Hence, success cannot be attained unless we follow the guiding principles established by the Creator.

*"This Book of the Law shall not depart from your mouth, but you shall read [and meditate on] it day and night, so that you may be careful to do [everything] in accordance with all that is written in it; for then you will make your way prosperous, and then you will be successful." **Joshua 1:8 AMP***

Attaining all-round success is hinged on thriving on the Word of God. Ponder and meditate on it day and night, making sure you practice everything written in it. Then you'll succeed. ᶜ

"Learn to be thankful for what you already have, while you pursue all that you want."

Jim Rohn

CHAPTER 12: THOU SHALT BE GRATEFUL

Like the popular saying that "the attitude of gratitude determines your altitude in life."

Practice the act of daily gratitude. For instance, you might think about or write down things you are thankful for each day.

Let Go of The Past

You won't be able to enjoy a better tomorrow if you are stuck in the past memories and constantly reliving setbacks or mistakes that happened a long time ago.

Unburden yourself from the weights of the past by letting go. We often hold on to the failed deals, the death of loved ones, the bad decisions that we made, mistakes in relationships, or the wrong turn in the wrong direction. No amount of guilt can change your past. However, each of those things can offer one or two lessons on how to move forward. Make peace with your past. Meditating on the good success we have had is a great way to overcome the harmful effects of living in the past.

Stop Worrying About Tomorrow

Worrying about the future will only sap out your energy, missing out on the present moment, which is where life is happening.

We worry about tomorrow; we get anxious about our survival, fearing something evil might happen. We try to predict, prepare, and plan for everything ahead of us. However, most things in life just happen, and the only thing we can do is be thankful and enjoy it, and make the best of it. No amount of anxiety can change your future. Let go of all the worries and anxieties, and the need to control and predict everything. Be Thankful!

*"Worrying is like paying the price you don't owe." **Mark Twain***

Don't Take It Personal

We tend to think that life is unfair when we fail or something bad happens.

Learn to look at challenges with a sense of humor and lightness of heart, this will allow you to overcome and move ahead quickly.

No one succeeds from this scratch. You will stumble, make mistakes, and fail; but the beauty of it is that you get the chance to try again, with more experience and confidence.

Appreciate What You Have

Grateful people live great lives. Being grateful doesn't necessarily mean being happy all the time. It simply means you are aware that no matter how hard or tough it may look, things will get better and you will come out strong on the other side. It means you are building the confidence that no matter how dark the night, joy will surely break forth in the morning.

If you are not great at gratitude, start a gratitude journal. Start by writing at least five things each day that you were grateful for. These include a positive experience you had, gift received, or people you interacted with. Gratitude helps you achieve life and career goals, making both your personal and professional lives more loving, productive, and enjoyable for you and everyone you touch. [a]

Final Thoughts

One of the major reasons people fail in life, work or business is that they refuse to acknowledge the Giver of success and fail to adhere to His instructions, laws, and principles of fulfilling true or good success.

*"And Pharaoh said, Who is the LORD, that I should obey his voice to let Israel go? I know not the LORD, neither will I let Israel go." **Exodus 5:2***

Ignorance of who God is has its consequences. It leads to failed dreams, untold struggles, toiling, stress, uneasiness, lack of peace and destruction. Most people have a limited knowledge of who the ***"I Am"*** is, they take Him as "one of the religious gods" that crazy and lazy fanatics cry to for succor or comfort.

He is the Creator of all things; you inclusive. He formed and shaped everything according to His purpose. He directs the affairs of all things in the universe and all galaxies. Everything is working according to His plan and timetable, in Him we live, move, and have our being. Without Him true success can't be attained, because He created you with intent, having an expected end in mind.

So, whatever we define as success shouldn't be in tangent with His will, plan and purpose for you. If you are successful in the wrong assignment, that would be tragic. It would be the greatest tragedy of your existence if you continue to walk and work in ignorance, oblivious of His plan and purpose for your life. God will never accept ignorance as an excuse for disobedience to His will.

Knowledge, however, is power. More so, the knowledge of the Most High God. It is the ultimate power.

How do we know God to the extent that we can draw maximum benefits from Him?

How do we avoid walking contrary to His will? God is the source of both temporal and eternal blessings. To know Him, you must first know Jesus. Matthew 11:27 says: "All things are delivered unto me of my Father; and no man knoweth the Son, but the Father; neither knoweth any man the Father, save the Son, and he to whomsoever the Son will reveal him."

Knowing Jesus Christ is knowing the mind of God and those who know their God shall be strong and do exploits. [a]

"He that covereth his sins shall not prosper: but whoso confesseth and forsaketh them shall have mercy." **Proverbs 28:13**

If you have read through this book but realize you've never had a personal relationship with Jesus Christ, please pray the following in faith:

Dear Father,

I believe that Jesus Christ was made manifest in the flesh to die for my sins and was raised from the dead that I might live forever. I come to you in need of forgiveness. Please forgive me for all my sins. I turn over my life completely to You.

Thank You for your saving grace and forgiving my sins. I ask you now to be my Lord, my Master, And My Personal Savior. I turn from my sinful ways to follow Jesus completely. I receive the free gift of salvation. Amen!

Notes

Chapter 3

a. *https://wikihow.com/Be-Successful*

b. *https://medium.com/@kashyapvartika/active-procrastination-can-lead-to-great success-in-your-life- 56ba77c74798*

c. *https://www.mindtools.com/pages/article/smartgoals.html*

d. *http://liveyourlegend.net/warren-buffets-5-steps-process-for-prioritizing-true-success-and-why-mostpeople-never-do-it/*

Chapter 8

a. *www.entrepreneur.com/article/231277*

b. *https://thriveglobal.com/stories/how-being-healthier-will-help-you-succeed/*

Chapter 10

a. *http://money.usnews.com/money/blogs/outsidevoices-careers/2014/12/10/the-top-10-skills-you-need-tobe-successful*

b. *http://www.entrepreneur.com/article/245086*

c. *http://money.usnews.com/money/blogs/outsidevoices-careers/2014/12/10/the-top-10-skills-you-need-to-be-successful*

d. *https://www.toolshero.com/psychology/principles-of-success*

Chapter 11

a. https://bible.com/1/pro.15:2.KJV

b. https://bible.com/97/pro.20:18.MSG

c. https://bible.com/bible/1588/jos.1.8.MSG

Chapter 12

a. https://www.entrepreneur.com/article/244867

Final Thoughts

a. Open Heavens Devotional. Friday 22nd of May 2020. That I May Know Him